THIS BOOK BELONGS TO:

MOLLY OSBORNE

YOUR TURN!

	A	B	C	D	E	F
1						
2						
3						
4						
5						
6						
7						

YOUR TURN!

	A	B	C	D	E	F
1						
2						
3						
4						
5						
6						
7						

YOUR TURN!

A B C D E F

1
2
3
4
5
6
7

YOUR TURN!

	A	B	C	D	E	F
1						
2						
3						
4						
5						
6						
7						

YOUR TURN!

	A	B	C	D	E	F
1						
2						
3						
4						
5						
6						
7						

YOUR TURN!

	A	B	C	D	E	F
1						
2						
3						
4						
5						
6						
7						

YOUR TURN!

	A	B	C	D	E	F
1						
2						
3						
4						
5						
6						
7						

YOUR TURN!

	A	B	C	D	E	F
1						
2						
3						
4						
5						
6						
7						

YOUR TURN!

	A	B	C	D	E	F
1						
2						
3						
4						
5						
6						
7						

A B C D E F

1

2

3

4

5

6

7

YOUR TURN!

	A	B	C	D	E	F
1						
2						
3						
4						
5						
6						
7						

YOUR TURN!

	A	B	C	D	E	F
1						
2						
3						
4						
5						
6						
7						

YOUR TURN!

	A	B	C	D	E	F
1						
2						
3						
4						
5						
6						
7						

YOUR TURN!

	A	B	C	D	E	F
1						
2						
3						
4						
5						
6						
7						

YOUR TURN!

	A	B	C	D	E	F
1						
2						
3						
4						
5						
6						
7						

YOUR TURN!

	A	B	C	D	E	F
1						
2						
3						
4						
5						
6						
7						

YOUR TURN!

	A	B	C	D	E	F
1						
2						
3						
4						
5						
6						
7						

YOUR TURN!

	A	B	C	D	E	F
1						
2						
3						
4						
5						
6						
7						

YOUR TURN!

	A	B	C	D	E	F
1						
2						
3						
4						
5						
6						
7						

YOUR TURN!

	A	B	C	D	E	F
1						
2						
3						
4						
5						
6						
7						

YOUR TURN!

	A	B	C	D	E	F
1						
2						
3						
4						
5						
6						
7						

YOUR TURN!

	A	B	C	D	E	F
1						
2						
3						
4						
5						
6						
7						

YOUR TURN!

	A	B	C	D	E	F
1						
2						
3						
4						
5						
6						
7						

YOUR TURN!

	A	B	C	D	E	F
1						
2						
3						
4						
5						
6						
7						

YOUR TURN!

	A	B	C	D	E	F
1						
2						
3						
4						
5						
6						
7						

YOUR TURN!

	A	B	C	D	E	F
1						
2						
3						
4						
5						
6						
7						

YOUR TURN!

	A	B	C	D	E	F
1						
2						
3						
4						
5						
6						
7						

YOUR TURN!

	A	B	C	D	E	F
1						
2						
3						
4						
5						
6						
7						

YOUR TURN!

A   B   C   D   E   F

1

2

3

4

5

6

7

YOUR TURN!

	A	B	C	D	E	F
1						
2						
3						
4						
5						
6						
7						

YOUR TURN!

	A	B	C	D	E	F
1						
2						
3						
4						
5						
6						
7						

Don't stop believing

Thank you for choosing this book.

I hope your child has enjoyed completing the activities in this book as much as I enjoyed creating it.

Your feedback is very important to me.

If you have encountered any issue with your book, such as printing errors, faulty binding, paper bleeding or any other issue, please do not hesitate to contact me at:

 happybooksforall@gmail.com

 /happybooksforall

 /happy.bookss

If you enjoyed this book, please consider leaving a review on the website. It takes a few minutes, but it would be so much appreciated. Reviews are a brilliant thing for small businesses like us – they are the best way to let other potential customers know about the book and your opinion about it. We encourage you to feel free to add photos of the interior and cover of this book in your review.

Thank you again for choosing this book.

© **Copyright 2020 - All rights reserved.**

You may not reproduce, duplicate or send the contents of this book without direct written permission from the author. You cannot hereby despite any circumstance blame the publisher or hold him or her to legal responsibility for any reparation, compensations, or monetary forfeiture owing to the information included herein, either in a direct or an indirect way.

Legal Notice: This book has copyright protection. You can use the book for personal purpose. You should not sell, use, alter, distribute, quote, take excerpts or paraphrase in part or whole the material contained in this book without obtaining the permission of the author first.

Disclaimer Notice: You must take note that the information in this document is for casual reading and entertainment purposes only. We have made every attempt to provide accurate, up to date and reliable information. We do not express or imply guarantees of any kind. The persons who read admit that the writer is not occupied in giving legal, financial, medical or other advice. We put this book content by sourcing various places.

Please consult a licensed professional before you try any techniques shown in this book. By going through this document, the book lover comes to an agreement that under no situation is the author accountable for any forfeiture, direct or indirect, which they may incur because of the use of material contained in this document, including, but not limited to, — errors, omissions, or inaccuracies.

www.ingramcontent.com/pod-product-compliance
Lightning Source LLC
Chambersburg PA
CBHW080401241225
37227CB00045B/1146